BuckGet.com –

How To Make Money and Earn a Living Online at

BuckGet.com for free -

Step By Step Quick Start Guide

Here are the Steps:

Step 1: Join BuckGet.com for free

Step 2: Post your microjobs at BuckGet.com for free

Step 3: Share and manage your microjobs at BuckGet.com for free

Step 4: Repeat from Step 2

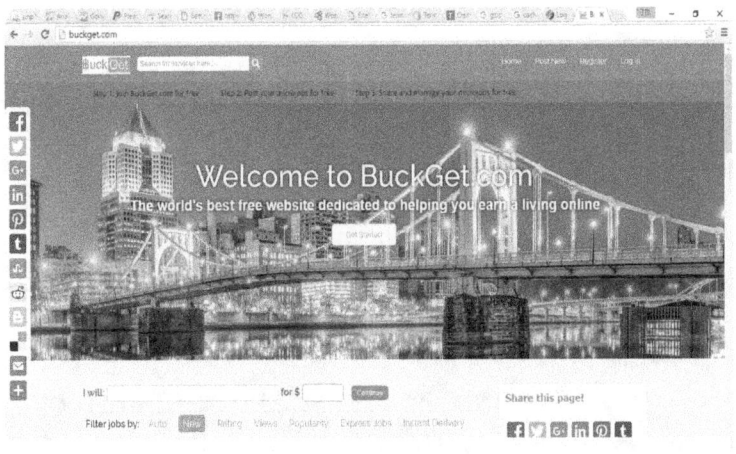

Step 1: Join BuckGet.com for free

Go to http://buckget.com/ , click on "Register" at

the top right, the "Get Started" button in the

middle of the home page or the "Step 1: Join

BuckGet.com for free" in the menu on the middle

left above the big picture to go to

http://buckget.com/wp-login.php?action=register

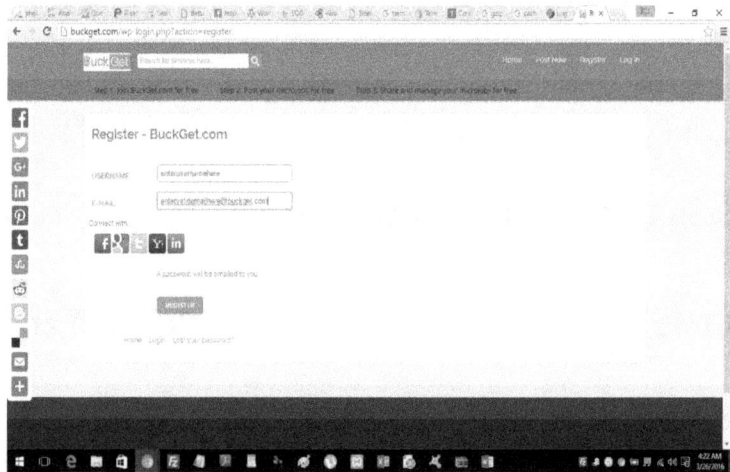

Once you are at http://buckget.com/wp-login.php?action=register , fill in your username with no spaces, special characters or capital letters, fill in your valid email address and click the "Register" button.

A password will be emailed to you. Please keep it handy. You will need it until/unless you decide to change it.

Go to your email, find the email BuckGet.com sent you (if it isn't in your inbox, check your spam folder and make sure you mark the email as "not spam" to receive emails from BuckGet.com), go back to http://buckget.com/ , click on "Log in" on the top right of the home page and enter your username and the password provided in the email.

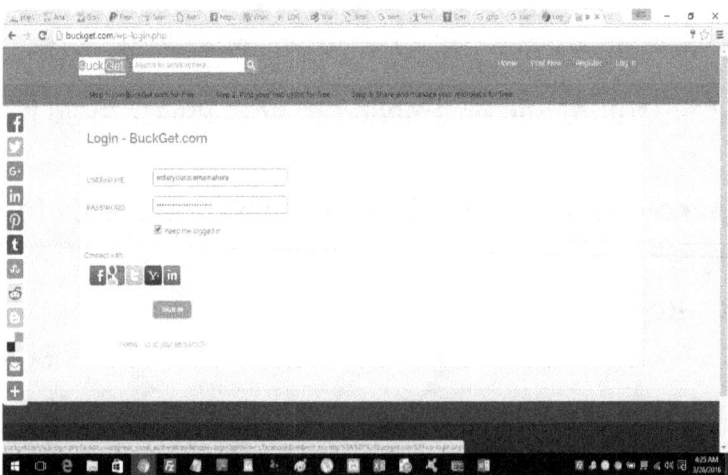

If you wish to register via social media, go to

http://buckget.com/wp-login.php?action=register

and click on the facebook, twitter, google, linkedin

or yahoo icon and follow the instructions. You will

be instantly signed up for BuckGet.com for free.

Step 2: Post your microjobs at BuckGet.com for

free

Once you are registered and logged in to BuckGet,

go to http://buckget.com/ and click on "Post New"

at the top right, the "Get Started" button in the

middle, the "Step 2: Post your microjobs at

BuckGet.com for free" in the menu on the middle

left above the big picture to go to

http://buckget.com/post-new-job/ .

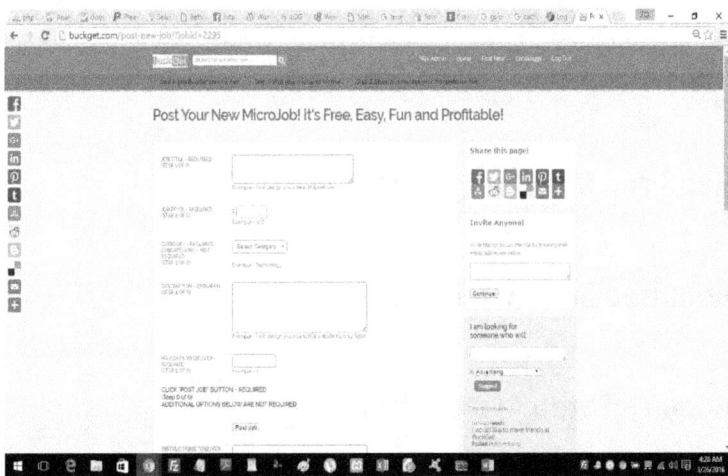

Once you are at http://buckget.com/post-new-job/ , you will see the title "Post Your New MicroJob! It's Free, Easy, Fun and Profitable!

There are six required steps and ten optional steps to posting a microjob:

Required Step 1: Job Title

Required Step 2: Job Price

Required Step 3: Category

Required Step 4: Description

Required Step 5: Max days to deliver

Required Step 6: Click the "Post Job" button.

That's it! You have just started an online business at BuckGet.com for free!

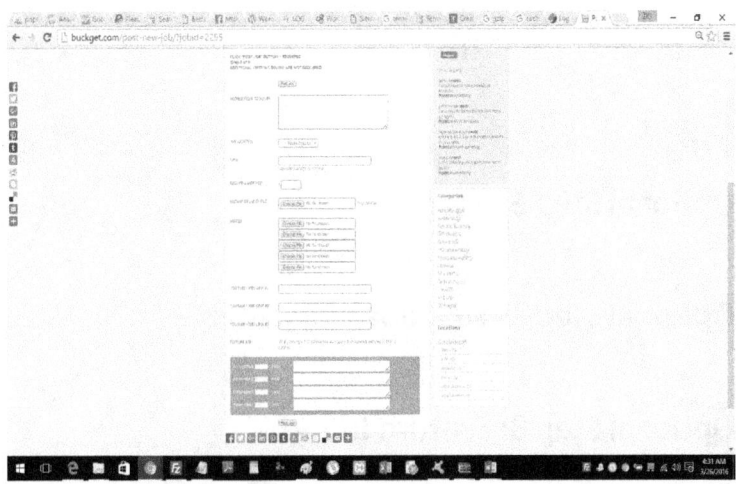

The optional steps are:

Optional Step 1: Instructions to buyer

Optional Step 2: Job location

Optional Step 3: Tags

Optional Step 4: Requires Shipping?

Optional Step 5: Instant delivery file

Optional Step 6: Images

Optional Step 7: YouTube video link

Optional Step 8: Feature Job

Optional Step 9: Extras

Required Step 10 or 6: Click the "Post Job" button.

If you chose to follow the additional optional

steps, that's it! You have just started an online

business at BuckGet.com for free!

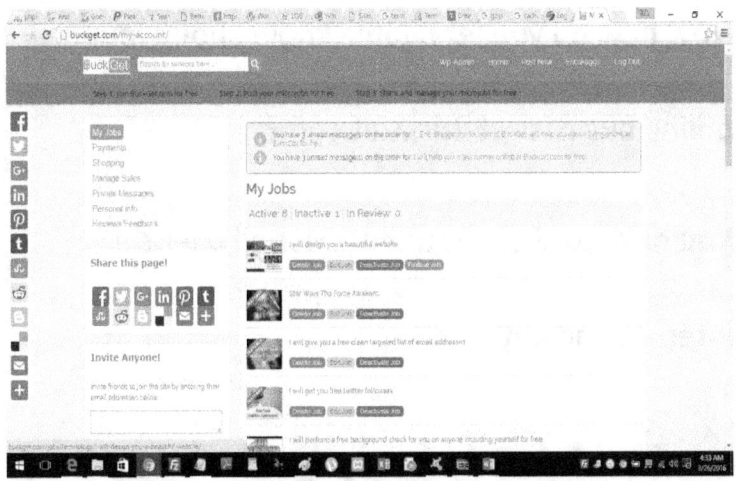

Step 3: Share and manage your microjobs at BuckGet.com for free.

You are logged in to BuckGet.com, you have just posted your first microjob at BuckGet.com and you have your online business started.

Now how do you let people know about your new

online business at BuckGet.com?

You have to share your business all over the

internet and beyond!

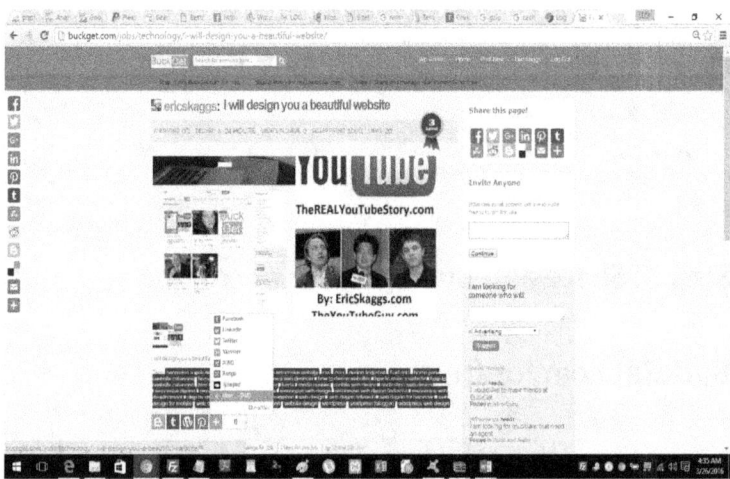

To share your online business with the world, click

on your username on the top right of any page at

BuckGet.com or in the pulldown menu, select

"Step 3: Share and manage your microjobs at

BuckGet.com for free" to go to

http://buckget.com/my-account/ .

Click on either the picture or the title of your

microjob. You will see icons for sharing your

business all over the internet on the sides and

bottom of your post.

You can share your business with your friends on facebook, twitter, google, linkedin, pinterest, tumblr, stumbleupon, reddit, blogger, delicious, email and if you click on the blue square icon with the white "plus" sign in it, you can share your business at over 300 places!

Take some time with this. This is the most important part of your new online business. I would recommend sharing your business at BuckGet with all the over 300 places listed.

Spend up to a week doing this. If you need to sign

up for different websites to share your business,

do it quickly.

You will get really good at this. It will have the

added benefit of giving you a broader reach on the

internet, which is very important if you wish to

expand and grow your online business.

At http://buckget.com/my-account/ next to your jobs, you will see options like delete job, edit job, deactivate job and feature job at all of your posts.

Do not be afraid to experiment with these, but remember that deleting jobs is permanent and deactivating jobs is temporary, so do not delete jobs unless you are absolutely sure that is what you want to do.

On the side of http://buckget.com/my-account/ ,

you will see options like my jobs, payments,

shopping, manage sales, private messages,

personal info and reviews/feedback.

This is where your notifications for your jobs, the

payments you receive, the items you have

purchased, the jobs you should perform, messages

from customers and potential customers, your

business profile and reviews and feedback that

you receive from customers.

Experiment with these settings. The only thing I would advise you to do is keep up with your orders and perform tasks in a timely fashion to make more money and develop a good reputation.

You should now be at least making money online, and you should be well on your way to earning a living online. Maybe someday, you will get rich online!

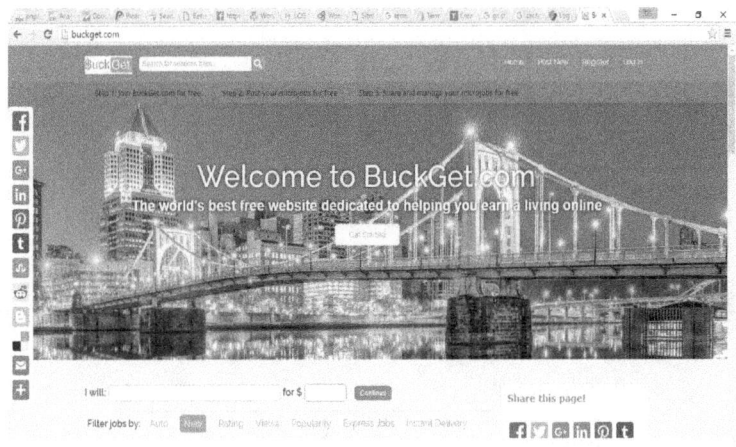

Step 4: Repeat from Step 2

Let me remind you of the steps:

Step 1: Join BuckGet.com for free

Step 2: Post your microjobs at BuckGet.com for

free

Step 3: Share and manage your microjobs at

BuckGet.com for free

Step 4: Repeat from Step 2

Keep posting new jobs, promoting them and

performing tasks. Don't give up! This should be

something you do every day and it is a good idea

to set a daily schedule to keep yourself on track.

Everybody is different, and do what works for you.

Just don't ever quit and you will be successful!

If you need anything at all, please contact me at

http://EricSkaggs.com , http://BuckGet.com/user-profile/ericskaggs and/or

http://BuckGet.com/members/ericskaggs.

You can also get assistance from BuckGet.com's nearly 4 million members/BuckGetters and growing at http://buckget.com/members/ .

And don't forget to invite your friends to join

BuckGet.com . They will thank you when they are

successful as well!

Thank you and Happy BuckGetting, BuckGetter!

EricSkaggs.com

Founder and Chief BuckGetter of BuckGet.com